Reach For The Stars

SUMMARY

Michael's new novel is called Reach for The Stars, a continuous story of Michaels's life and career as an entrepreneur.

Michaels's many creative ideas, and willingness to help others in their careers made him a successful businessman.

Michael is a creative individual and a total perfectionist in whatever he sets out to do. Michael would not give up until he accomplished his goals, of what his career is today.

Michael has developed many businesses with his company The Kilmartin Organization Inc, a worldwide company since 1972.

Michael will never give up or retire from his business, even through the hard work, late-night hours, and years of researching, and continuing education, even though

Michael is well into his seventies. Michaels's Motto is, "You never graduate because education, business, technology, and life change from day to day"

Michael has accomplished many things in his lifetime, and he continues to build a lifetime of dreams that have come true.

Michael has amazed many people in business, and they have asked him many times how he did it, and his answer is "a lifetime in believing in myself and my goal.

Contents

1

2

3

4

5

6

7

8

9

10

Dedication

I Michael Lee Kilmartin hereby dedicate my novels and short stories to my daughters Kristi and Lori. They inspired me to write my stories way back when they were just children. I can remember when I read my stories to them while taking a nap and at bedtime, how they became so excited when I read to them about aliens, and monsters that I had written for them.

About The Author

Michael did not come from a rich family; in fact, he came from a broken family at the age of six. Where his mother and father divorced, and the courts ordered

Michael's Father and mother. Were ordered to have them sent to foster care. Michael and his brothers then were placed in several foster homes, and a boy's home for over six years, until their mother remarried. Michael became an introverted shy child from the many places he was sent to as a child and making his growing-up years a nightmare and difficult for him to talk to people.

From the Author

Hello everyone, my name is Michael Lee Kilmartin. I was born in the United States. I am a Scotsman and an Irishman. I grew up in a little town called Moorpark, California. My career for the last forty years has been as an entrepreneur, optimist, and philanthropist, and now an author with my company The Kilmartin Organization Inc.

Reach For The Stars

1

Michael did not come from a rich family when he started his business career in 1972. He was just ten years old when he became a paperboy, Michael was born in Oceanside, California in the City of San Diego.

Michael's father was a military man; Marines, and Air force for over thirty years. Michael's parents divorced when he was just five years old.

Michael and his two brothers Pat and Dennis were placed in several foster homes, and then a boy's home for over six years.

Michael's mother remarried, and Michael and his brothers were then brought home to a small country town called Moorpark, California.

Michael went to an elementary school, called Flory elementary and a high school called Moorpark High.

Michael is a very ambitious, and motivated creative individual. He loved to draw and paint and as a child, he painted and drew many pictures for the local fairs, and his schools.

Michael loved making many model cars, planes, and boats that he entered at state fairs and hobby shows.

Michael received many trophies and ribbons for his work. Michael created a logo for his high school-class jackets and sweaters.

Michael worked in many jobs in and around Moorpark; box boy, grocery clerk, fruit picker, paperboy, and newspaper dealer.

Michael's high school years were the best years of his life. Michael excelled in track, football, and basketball. Michael's favorite sport was Track where he won many medals, ribbons, and trophies.

Michael set many school records at Moorpark High as a successful long-distance runner.

Michael's success in track was awarded the State Title for the State of California for three consecutive years.

Michael was then awarded and received a four-year college scholarship to Cal Poly State University upon graduation.

Reach For The Stars

2

Michael loved his teen years; dancing the rock n roll of the sixties with Dick Clark, American Band Stand, Wolf Man Jack, and Casey Kasim of America's Top 40.

Michael in 1965 applied for a job with the Vons's Grocery Company, where he learned the art of retailing when he started as a box boy and worked his way up to become a manager while he attended Ventura College.

Michael moved from his home in Moorpark to Ventura, California at the age of eighteen, where he continued his college education at Ventura College, and then on to Ventura College of Law upon graduation.

Michael Say's with technology growing as fast as it has, you never graduate, there is always something more to learn no matter how old you are.

Michael worked for a company called Bradshaw Inc, a food broker where he became a salesman.

He learned the business from bottom to top, in the art of salesmanship, writing orders and creating contracts, merchandising, and marketing as a territory manager, and as an international food broker. Selling promotional products with Bradshaw; Tree Sweet orange juice is frozen and juice, green giant foods, Swift sausage, Alex Tamales, and nonfood products Milita Coffee products to all the retail stores.

Michael's career with Bradshaw was a success, and he was promoted to district manager for the city of San Diego, California. Michael received many sales awards and letters of achievement from Bradshaw.

Reach For The Stars

3

Michael created the first company in 1972, which he started from the ground up called Sales Unlimited & Associates, a broker, and a manufacturers representative, just like Bradshaw Inc.

He started his company in San Diego, where he lived, and went to San Diego State University, at night while building his business.

Michael went out to meet many businesses with unknown product names and contracted with them. which were unknown at the beginning of his company.

His lines were called Jason Cosmetics a lotion and cream line, Orly Nail Care, a nail care product line, Vidal Sassoon a shampoo and hair care line, Maji Nail a nail care product line, Aprinique skin care a lotion and skin line, Hang Ten a tanning line, and IBG a professional hair care line on contract and straight commission.

Michael enjoyed selling Hang Ten up and down the coast to retailers in California.

Michael was now growing with the establishment of the lines he represented to the retailers, and in warehousing in Simi Valley, whereas he originally started from his garage in Simi Valley.

Surfing was one of Michael's favorite hobbies "Yes, Michael was a surfer" with his sun-bleached hair and that golden tan with those knobby knees back in the sixties.

Reach For The Stars

4

Michael incorporated his business in 1975 and renamed his company Kilmartin Enterprises Inc. He then became a distributor of many of the products that he represented and was able to distribute them to all retailers worldwide.

Michael then applied for his realtor license to learn the art of real estate and leasing for his company. Where he handled all leasing contracts for his companies, and with his properties to buy and sell as an investor.

Michael purchased many properties and built a portfolio of over thirty properties; duplexes and single-family homes in California, Arizona, and Nevada.

Michael sold many businesses of all types as a commercial acquisitions *broker with his company Kilmartin Enterprises Inc. restaurants; mom and pop, night clubs, manufacturing, and commercial buildings, and Michael became a mortgage broker to finance his businesses, residents, and commercial properties.*

To learn the art of financing with his company to be able to finance his investments with the company he started called Financial Bankers & Associates another dba of Kilmartin Enterprises Inc.

Michael then developed his business in the growing stage and hired salespeople, managers, office personnel, and warehouse personnel to package and ship the company orders as the company grew nationally and internationally.

Reach For The Stars

5

Michael traveled to all the states in the United States and abroad selling and contracting his products to build and present his labels to retailers worldwide.

Michael 1980 continued his education at Kenra Laboratories, Los Angeles, California. To study the art of chemical formulation to learn how to formulate and manufacture skin care products.

Michael's first venture in manufacturing was with a line of products that he created and trademarked called Natures Earth. A successful natural skincare line company, and line of natural organic skincare products.

Michael formulated, and designed the packaging and logos for his skincare line and created many skin care products, over four hundred natural; wrinkle creams, day & night creams, facial scrubs, skin fresheners, body wash, shampoos and conditioners, hair sprays, hand and body lotions, body oils, tanning lotions, Aloe Vera gels, and first aid products.

Michael contracted with many manufacturers' agents nationally, and

Bradshaw became one of those companies.

Michael hired and contracted with international sales representatives and brokers nationally to sell his products to China, Japan, Russia, Germany, Sweden, and Mexico.

The company moved to a larger building for manufacturing, where Michael created a laboratory and a distribution center for Nature's Earth line.

Michael built two manufacturing plants. for his company from the ground up. Nature's Earth became a worldwide skincare line.

Reach For The Stars

6

In 1985 Michael created a chain of health food stores called Nature's Earth Nutrition Centers, and Michael's mother became his first store manager.

The stores stocked a complete line of health food products and national brand vitamins. Michael created a vitamin line with the Nature's Earth label.

Michael manufactured and created many product lines that he trademarked, designed, and packaged; Natures Earth, Basic Shave, Derma Flex, Follex hair care, Oil of Life, Feminine Shave, Oil of Love, Kristi Lee Nail Care, Pet Life International, and a skincare line with Michael's name. Michael sold and contracted and distributed to all the retailers, department stores, grocery, drug stores, pharmacies, mass merchandisers, distributors, and wholesalers nationally.

Reach For The Stars

6

Michael 1998 created the Dollar Store Division. The company grew rapidly in contracting and selling millions of bottles and jars of skin care products to retailers.

To dollar stores, distributors, wholesalers, Pic & Save, Dollar Tree, Dollar General, Bargain wholesale, and the 99 cent-only stores nationally.

Michael created a company called Financial Bankers Inc. a full-service finance company.

Kilmartin Enterprises was renamed The Kilmartin Organization Inc, and then he sold the company in 1999, and he continued his career as the president of Financial Bankers & Associates.

Michael 2014 returned to his college education at Moorpark College to learn more about his many other interests

They are art, illustration, painting, and creative writing. 2014 Michael became a writer and a poet.

He created a website in 2014 called the "Michael Lee Kilmartin Collection" where he displays many of his works.

Michael's career has been through many good times and sad

times. Losing his younger brother Richard in 2000, and his brother Patrick in 2015.

Reach For The Stars

7

Michael created a law firm in Mexico "KC Law" a law practice in Mexico and California. Michael contracted, and helped many people with their success in migrating to the United States.

He helped the Mexican people with applications, required documents, and briefs to meet with the immigration departments, to receive visas to be able to come to America.

Michael studied Spanish at the University of Mexico. Michael's writing career became a success, and he became an author.

Reach For The Stars

8

Michael in 2014 published his first novel called "My Encounter, We Are Not Alone" and he continued to write many novels and children's books that are now sold worldwide.

On Amazon, Google, Barnes & Noble, eBay, Walmart, Target, and many bookstores worldwide.

Michael has published many books in children's stories, science fiction, mystery, romance, thrillers, suspense, horror, westerns, and comic books.

Some of the many titles and series he has created; My Encounter Series, Shorty & Sparky's Adventures series, The Entrepreneur Series, The FBI series, My Vampire Tales series, The Michael Says Series, The

Wolfman Series, The Baby Blue Series, The Boot Hill Series, The Gunslinger series, The Jackson's Detective Series, Tommy Rockets comic book series, Bucky's comic book series, The Bad Boy comics series, and Cool Dudes Adventures. Michael Says he is working hard in becoming a writer and author and his goal is to be that great writer.

Michael believes in "practice makes perfect" and maybe one day he too will become the next Doctor Seuss.

Reach For The Stars

9

Michael is a Star Trekkie and he says "is it not amazing how many books and movies are about Outerspace and that has now become a reality? Like the Flash Gordon, and the Star Trek Series.

Michael looks up to the stars and wonders who may be looking back. Michael says he has his track shoes back on and he is off and running to the winner's circle.

Michael says "I will never retire, why retire when I am having so much fun helping people and watching them be successful?

I like doing what I love doing best and that is being an entrepreneur, explorer, and writing my favorite stories, and looking for the next adventure"

*Your friend and mine,
Michael Lee Kilmartin*

Reach for The Stars

THE END

www.ingramcontent.com/pod-product-compliance
Lightning Source LLC
Chambersburg PA
CBHW050315220526
45465CB00005B/2002